•THE GERMAN AIRCRAFT CARRIER•

GRAF ZEPPELIN

SIEGFRIED BREYER

The final preparations for the launch of aircraft carrier "A" are made: the last of the scaffolding surrounding the ship is being removed and the christening pulpit in the foreground is being built.

Schiffer Military History
Atglen, PA

BIBLIOGRAPHY (Selected)

Breyer, Koop: *Von der EMDEN zur TIRPITZ. Vol. 1*, Munich 1980.

Dülffer: *Weimar, Hitler und die Marine*, Düsseldorf 1973.

Gröner: *Die deutschen Kriegsschiffe 1815-1945, Vol. 1*, Koblenz 1982.

Hadeler: *Flugzeugschiffe*, Munich 1939.

Hadeler: *Der Flugzeugträger*, Munich 1968.

Hadeler: *Kriegsschiffbau*, Darmstadt 1968.

Hadeler: *Mündliche und schriftliche Mitteilungen sowie Bildmaterial zu GRAF ZEPPELIN an den Verfasser.*

Kens, Nowarra: *Die deutschen Flugzeuge 1933-1945*, Munich 1977.

Nowarra: *Me 109 (Vol. 2), "The Weapon Arsenal" series, Vol. 87*, Friedberg 1984.

Stein: *Ju 87, "The Weapon Arsenal" series, Vol. 57*, Friedberg 1979.

Salewski: *Die deutsche Seekriegsleitung 1933-1945, 3 Vol.*, Munich 1970, 1973, 1975.

Wagner (Ed.): *Die Lagevorträge des Oberbefehlshabers der Kriegsmarine 1939-1945*, Munich 1971.

Translated from the German by Dr. Edward Force, Central Connecticut State University.

Copyright © 1989 by Schiffer Publishing.
Library of Congress Catalog Number: 90-060481.

Printed in China
ISBN: 0-88740-242-9

This title originally published as, "Flugzeugtrager Graf Zeppelin," by Podzun-Pallas-Verlag, 6360 Friedberg 3 (Dorheim), © 1988, ISBN 3-7909-0334-5.

Published by Schiffer Publishing Ltd
4880 Lower Valley Road
Atglen, PA 19310
Phone: (610) 593-1777; Fax: (610) 593-2002
E-mail: Info@schifferbooks.com
Please visit our web site catalog at **www.schifferbooks.com**

In Europe, Schiffer books are distributed by Bushwood Books
6 Marksbury Avenue Kew Gardens
Surrey TW9 4JF England
Phone: 44 (0) 20-8392-8585; Fax: 44 (0) 20-8392-9876
E-mail: info@bushwoodbooks.co.uk
Free postage in the UK. Europe: air mail at cost.

This book may be purchased from the publisher.
Include $3.95 for shipping. Please try your bookstore first.
We are always looking for people to write books on new and related subjects.
If you have an idea for a book please contact us at the above address.
You may write for a free catalog.

These were the first "guiding pictures" for the German aircraft carrier design: At the top, the British COURAGEOUS: this and its sister ship GLORIOUS (both sunk by German naval forces in the first year of the war) were regarded as the most perfected of their time. In the center is the FURIOUS, which was opened to visitors during the "Navy Week" at Portsmouth in 1935. Below is the Japanese AKAGI, which was opened to a visit from a three-man German commission in the autumn of 1935. Soon the Germans turned away from these "examples" and created a largely independent design.

CONSTRUCTION HISTORY

When a new type of warship, the aircraft carrier, came into existence after World War I, it could not yet be suspected that a quarter-century later this type would surpass and finally replace the battleship, which until then had been regarded as the "nucleus" of every high-sea fleet. At that time the aircraft carrier was still regarded as a kind of auxiliary warship, and certainly as a satellite of the battleship, to which it could be assigned for its protection. Only a few far-seeing naval officers considered the possibility of offensive carrier warfare, and they were stationed, as could be said, at indefensible positions. The opposition of those circles who continued to see the battleship as the "non plus ultra" and were willing to concede, at most, reconnaissance service and defensive possibilities to the carrier, was too great. But since the new type of warship was at hand, the great sea powers did not give up on it, but at first they did very little to promote its further development. Meanwhile, time worked in favor of the airplane: with the increase in aircraft performance, the tactical standpoints toward a future sea war changed, and the aircraft carrier gradually gained importance.

The German Navy was denied participation in this development, for the conditions of the Treaty of Versailles allowed neither the building of aircraft carriers nor, in fact, the possession of military aircraft. The military value of the aircraft carrier had been recognized by knowledgeable German naval officers, and indeed, relatively long before the German military buildup that followed Hitler's coming to power. After the development of the Luftwaffe as the third branch of the military had begun, the navy also considered this new type of warship. The development, as first overwhelmingly theoretical, found its first lasting expression when, about as 1933 gave way to 1934, the construction department of the navy was commissioned to prepare a study design for an aircraft carrier. It was based on the following military requirements:

Water displacement approximately 20,000 tons;
Speed 33 knots;
50 to 60 aircraft;
Armament eight 20.3 cm guns, plus strong anti-aircraft firepower, armor and interior protection according to the established norms for light cruisers.

This task was hard enough: No kind of experience was available, and the reference material on the aircraft carriers of other fleets was limited to the extent of knowledge contained in the current literature on the subject. Yet these foreign carriers had to be looked to as models, simply in order to get some knowledge of the basic principles. With this highly incomplete and insufficient material, the design director, at that time the 36-year-old naval architect, Dipl.Ing. Wilhelm Hadeler, had to feel his way forward step by step to the completion of the task. The Luftwaffe at first regarded itself as unable to collaborate because it was boundlessly over-

burdened by its hectic buildup; it was not even in a position to provide the navy with data on the dimensions of the carrier aircraft to be involved, data that were needed in order to determine the size of hangars and elevators.

Despite these stumbling blocks, the constructor was able to bring the study design to a definite conclusion in the course of a year. To be sure, the most important question—whether the task was completed purposefully—still remained open for the time being. All of the established requirements could be met: it must be noted that the eight 20.3 cm guns had been replaced by the same number of 15 cm guns. There were also ten 10.5 cm anti-aircraft guns and numerous machine weapons. In general, a displacement of about 23,000 tons and a speed of 35 knots could be calculated. Of the original model of this study design, the British COURAGEOUS class, there remained only a fighter takeoff deck from the uppermost hangar over the forecastle.

Design director for German carrier construction was Naval Chief Architect Dipl.Ing. Wilhelm Hadeler. He died on December 3, 1987, at the age of ninety.

The model of the carrier according to the stage of design in 1938, provided by the construction department of the naval high command; the unsatisfactorily planned sixth 10.5 cm double anti-aircraft unit—its position was intended to be before the two forward ones—is not yet included here.

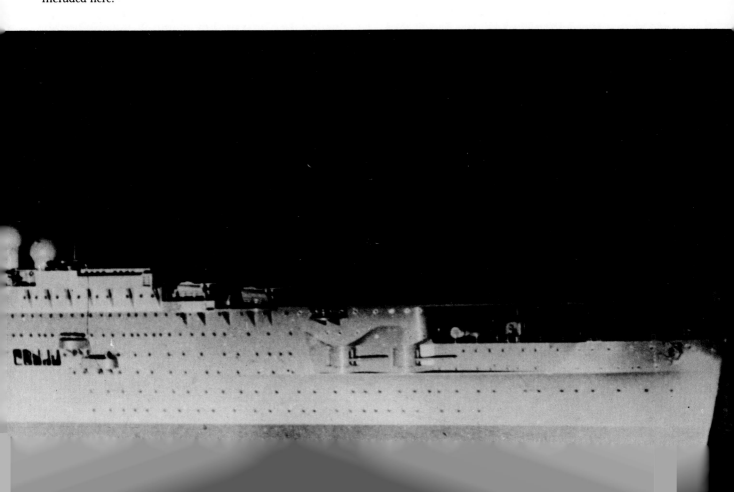

When the heavy cruiser BLUCHER was launched on June 8, 1937, the aircraft carrier "A", laid on the parallel slipway at Kiel half a year earlier, was still in its first stages of construction. Here it has not yet risen above the scaffolding that surrounds it, but a few months later it would tower over them.

The most important result of this study design, though, was that the involved units of the navy had, in the approximately 14 months of its development, acquired a conception of what was to be expected qualitatively and quantitatively of a carrier in terms of fighting value, and how many difficulties still had to be overcome until a usable design had been achieved. Accomplishing this had become necessary much earlier than even optimists had foreseen. As early as June 18, 1935 the way was opened for German aircraft carriers: on this day the German-British fleet agreement was signed, setting the future strength of the German Navy at 35% of the existing British warship tonnage, and applying to all types of ships. For aircraft carriers—based on what Britain had at that time—the allowance was 38,500 tons, meaning two designs of 19,250 tons each.

Revising the study design to fit this minor limitation proved to be not particularly difficult.

Under the decisively changed political aspects, the first German aircraft carrier (it was given the budgetary and construction designation "A") could be included in the 1936 fiscal year, with a second ("B") following in the 1938 fiscal year. The final design was very similar to the study design. At this time, though, the importance of the carrier-based aircraft with the impact of their primary weapons had not yet emerged, for as in wide circles of the great foreign navies, the Germans too did not see the actual nature of this new type of warship in such terms as they really should have: they had not yet recognized that its main weapon was simply the airplane. Instead, they stressed the artillery (which was regarded as the main factor of fighting value), which they upgraded by doubling the number of guns.

The high-rising carrier's hull is decorated with garlands in preparation for its launching.

A look at the carrier, ready for launching, from the other side. Under the overhanging flight deck qne can see the casemate openings in which the two forward port 15-cm double gun mounts were to be housed.

December 8, 1938: Hitler enters the shipyard with a large retinue to take part for the third time in the launch of a great German warship. Here he inspects the naval honor guard standing alongside the carrier. Next to him are Admiral-General Dr. h.c. Raeder as Commander of the Navy, behind him Field Marshal Hermann Göring as Commander of the Luftwaffe. At the upper edge of the picture the overhang of the after 15 cm casemate battery can be seen.

Meanwhile the Luftwaffe had also begun to get involved in the developmental work. At their request, the fighter launching deck patterned after that of the British COURAGEOUS was to be eliminated. During this work, a high construction official of the K-Office was sent to "Navy Week" in England in order to have a look at the British aircraft carrier "Furious", which had been opened to the public. But this visit brought very little useful information. Negotiations with the Japanese Navy were more successful. In the fall of 1935 the Japanese allowed a German commission to observe their aircraft carrier AKAGI. In the process, the commission was given about 100 special plans, including blueprints, in the area of the flight system. But the total results here too were not as productive as had been hoped. On the basis of what had been seen there, only a third—the central—aircraft elevator was added, along with a few less important modifications. But the visit to Japan had made one thing clear—and it proved to be extremely important and valuable: it was made clear that the Germans were on the right track.

The Aircraft Carriers of Foreign Navies on the Eve of World War II

Name	Year Launched	Tons	Knots	No. of planes	Final disposition
Great Britain					
Courageous[2]	1928	18,600	31	48	Torpedoed by German U 29 in North Atlantic 9/17/1939
Glorious[2]	1928	18,600	31	48	Sunk by artillery of German battleships Scharnhorst & Gneisenau in North Sea 6/8/1940
Furious[2]	1918	19,100	31	33	Dismantled 1948
Argus	1918	14,000	20.2	20	Dismantled 1946
Eagle[1]	1920	22,600	24	21	Torpedoed by German U 73 in Mediterranean 11/28/1942
Hermes	1924	10,850	25	15	Sunk by Japanese air-craft in Indian Ocean 4/9/1942
Ark Royal	1938	22,000	30.7	72	Torpedoed by German U 81 in Mediterranean 11/14/1941
Under construction					
Illustrious	1940	23,000	31	72	Dismantled 1956
Victorious	1940	23,000	31	72	Dismantled 1969
Formidable	1940	23,000	31	72	Dismantled 1953
Indomitable	1941	23,000	31	72	Dismantled 1955
Implacable	1944	26,000	32.5	72	Dismantled 1955
Indefatigable	1944	26,000	32.5	72	Dismantled 1956
USA					
Saratoga[2]	1927	33,000	34	90	Sunk as atom bomb target at Bikini 7/25/1946
Lexington[2]	1927	33,000	34	90	Sunk by Japanese air-craft in Coral Sea, 5/8/1942
Yorktown	1938	19,900	34	100	Sunk by Japanese air-craft at Midway, 6/7/1942
Enterprise	1937	19,900	34	100	Dismantled 1958
Ranger	1934	14,500	29.5	86	Dismantled 1947
Under Construction					
Hornet	1941	20,000	34	100	Sunk by Japanese air-craft at Santa Cruz Islands 10/27/1942
Wasp	1940	14,700	29.5	86	Torpedoed by Japanese U-boat south of the Solomons 9/15/1942

Name	Year Launched	Tons	Knots	No. of planes	Final disposition

Japan

Name	Year Launched	Tons	Knots	No. of planes	Final disposition
Hosho	1922	7,470	25	21	Dismantled 1947
Kaga[1]	1928	26,900	23	80	Sunk by US aircraft at Midway 6/4/1942
Akagi[2]	1927	26,900	28.5	60	Sunk by US aircraft at Midway 6/5/1942
Ryujo	1933	10,600	29	48	Sunk by US aircraft off Solomons 8/24/1942
Hiryu	1939	17,300	34.5	73	Sunk by US aircraft at Midway 6/5/1942
Soryu	1937	15,900	34.5	73	Sunk by US aircraft at Midway 6/4/1942

Under Construction

Name	Year Launched	Tons	Knots	No. of planes	Final disposition
Shokaku	1941	25,675	34	84	Torpedoed by US U-boat in Philippine Sea 6/19/1944
Zuikaku	1941	25,675	34	84	Sunk by US aircraft in Leyte Gulf 10/25/1944
Shoho	1942	11,262	28	30	Sunk by US aircraft in Coral Sea 5/8/1942
Zuiho	1940	11,262	28	30	Sunk by US aircraft in Leyte Gulf 10/25/1944

France

Name	Year Launched	Tons	Knots	No. of planes	Final disposition
Bearn[1]	1926	22,146	21	40	Dismantled 1967

Under Construction

Name	Year Launched	Tons	Knots	No. of planes	Final disposition
Joffre	—	18,000	33	40	Unfinished, dismantled
Painleve	—	18,000	33	40	Unfinished, dismantled

[1]Begun as a battleship.
[2]Begun or completed as a battle cruiser.

All other ships were built new as carriers.

The christening is completed, the covers have fallen away from the name boards and coat of arms, the ship goes into motion. On the next slipway (left) is the hull of the supply ship "C", the later FRANKEN (exactly six months were to go by until her launching). Easy to see here is the bow bulge of the carrier (the supply ship under construction shows a very similar form).

GRAF ZEPPELIN at the moment when the stern is afloat. This moment presents the hardest test of a newly-built ship in terms of its longitudinal firmness: while the stern and middle of the ship are already floating in "soft" water, the bow is still on the "hard" slipway, so that different pressures affect the ship and subject its frame to extremely great pressure.

After the design had reached its end for the time being, toward the end of 1935, and been approved by the commander of the navy, the Deutsche Werke Kiel AG—to which the ongoing construction had already been entrusted—received the contract on November 16, 1935 to build the aircraft carrier "A." This shipyard, though, was still working at capacity on the construction of other warships—the battleship GNEISENAU, the heavy cruiser BLUCHER, destroyers Z 1 to 4, U-boats 13 to 16 and supply ship FRANKEN—and its slipways were still full. For that reason, the construction of the carrier could proceed without haste up to the point of laying the keel.

On December 28, 1936 the carrier's keel was laid on Slipway 1 (from which the battleship GNEISENAU had been launched twenty days before). Almost exactly two years later, on December 8, 1938, it was launched and christened with the name GRAF ZEPPELIN.

For the second aircraft carrier ("B"), the contract for building the machinery had already been given on February 11, 1935, to the Friedrich Krupp Germania Shipyard in Kiel; the contract for the construction of the carrier itself followed on November 16, 1935. But the keel-laying could take place only in the latter half of 1938—after the launch of the heavy cruiser PRINZ EUGEN—because only this slipway was suitable for building the carrier. The work on it proceeded deliberately slowly, in order to take into consideration, if possible, experience gained from the GRAF ZEPPELIN. By the time the war began, the lower framework had risen only to the platform deck. According to peacetime planning, launching had been foreseen for July 1, 1940, and the earliest date of completion as December 1941. Two additional carriers, "C" and "D"—likewise according to peacetime conditions—were to be built at the Germania Shipyard and Deutsche Werke Kiel respectively, beginning in April of 1941 and being put into service by July of 1944.

The work on the GRAF ZEPPELIN made normal progress during the course of 1939. In August of 1939 it was seen that its completion in the last weeks of 1940 could be planned on. When the war broke out, the carrier was about 85% finished; the machinery was already installed and the boilers prepared, and only a few auxiliary machines, already available, were not yet installed. In all probability, the sea testing could begin in the winter of 1940-41. The 15 cm guns were already in place too, though their controls were still lacking. After the war began, work on the GRAF ZEPPELIN continued on schedule at first, but it was delayed soon afterward because of the increased production of U-boats (in terms of their levels of priority, the carriers were always ranked in last place—up to the beginning of the war, the order of priority had been: battleships, U-boats, destroyers, cruisers, aircraft carriers). Finally, on April 29, 1940 the commander of the navy himself suggested that the work be halted, because the carrier—even if it could be put in service on schedule, toward the end

A view of the GRAF ZEPPELIN from the other side. On the flight deck, the raised sections in which the catapult rails are attached can be seen.

of the year—was not ready for use in terms of artillery:

The 15 cm guns had already been removed and taken to Norway to strengthen the coast defenses there, the anti-aircraft guns had already been sent elsewhere, and the completion of the firing system had been delayed because of the delivery of such systems to the Soviet Union under the terms of the 1939 treaty with that country. On July 6, 1940 the GRAF ZEPPELIN was towed to Gotenhafen to get her away from the increasing danger of air attack. There she served as a floating storehouse for the navy's hardwood supplies. Early in the summer of 1941—just before the attack on the Soviet Union—she was moved to Stettin, where she was moored on June 21. This measure had been decided on because of expected Soviet air raids. When none took place, the carrier was taken back to Gotenhafen; on November 11 she passed Swinemunde in tow, on course for Gotenhafen.

Work on her sister ship "B"—to which postwar literature often gives the name of PETER STRASSER, a purely speculative rumor—had already been stopped on September 19, 1939. The material already built was broken up by an Essen firm beginning on February 28, 1940 and put to other uses.

The **GRAF ZEPPELIN**, fully afloat, shortly before dropping the bow anchor.

After the carrier has been brought to a stop, auxiliary craft help to handle its anchor cables and tugboats provide towlines.

Taken in tow by three tugboats, the GRAF ZEPPELIN is brought to the equipping pier.

The stern of the carrier. The supports of the rear flight-deck overhang and the two parallel spade rudders, extending just above the waterline, can be seen clearly.

Another view of the carrier's hull, giving an impression of massiveness. Here the openings on the sides in which the ship's boats would be located can be seen.

THE SHIP'S HULL

The ship's hull was divided into nineteen watertight compartments. This very narrow division corresponded to the usual norms for large German naval ships. Below water, the prow ended in a bulge (Taylor pear), by which the friction resistance was supposed to be reduced measurably. In terms of construction technology, the GRAF ZEPPELIN was one of the most interesting newly-built German warships. The carrier was laid out an "island type", meaning that all the superstructure was concentrated in one "island" on the starboard side. To equalize the weight of the island, the hangar decks and flight deck were set .8 meters to port of the ship's longitudinal axis; for that reason the outer skin had more of an overhang to port than to starboard. The GRAF ZEPPELIN originally was to have the almost vertical prow then customary in German warship building. In 1940 this was replaced by a so-called Atlantic prow, in order to improve seaworthiness; this construction effected a lengthening of the ship's hull by 5.2 meters. The GRAF ZEPPELIN was relatively well armored; the armor more or less corresponded to the norms for modern light cruisers. The thicknesses were as follows:

Side protection (waterline): Astern 60 to 80 mm, amidships 100 mm, forward 60 to 80 mm, bow protection 25 mm.

Horizontal protection (armor deck): Horizontal 40 mm, slopes 60 mm, over the rudder room 60 mm, forward 20 mm.

Flight deck: 20 mm (up to 45 mm in the areas around the elevators).

Bulkheads (in place of torpedo bulkheads): 20 mm.

Armor (transverse) bulkheads: Rib 10: 80 mm, rib 21, 25: 60 mm, rib 56.5: 60 mm (only over the bulkhead), rib 176: 60 mm (only over the bulkhead), rib 218: 80 mm.

Bridge: Chartroom etc. 17 mm, artillery control position 17 mm, anti-aircraft control positions 14 mm. Command post up to 150 mm.

Other protection: Cable passages 12 mm, side watch positions 12 mm, magazine 12 mm, gratings in air shafts

and smokestacks 100 mm.
Artillery: 15 cm casemates 20 mm, 15 cm shields 30 mm,
10.5 cm shields 10 mm.

As armoring material, the alloys "Wh" (Wotan
hard) and "Ww" (Wotan soft), then very new, were
widely used.

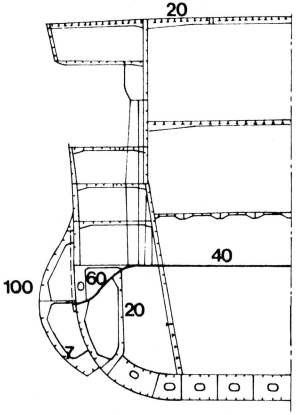

Drawing of the main rib plane (Rib 137). The numbers
indicate the thickness of armor plate in millimeters.

The construction harbor of the Deutsche Werke Kiel AG, photographed in the summer of 1939. At the left rear, under the crane at the equipping pier, is the aircraft carrier GRAF ZEPPELIN. Tied up to the outside of the pier is the supply ship "C" (FRANKEN), launched on July 8, 1939. In the foreground are torpedo boats and minesweepers (some of them in drydocks), and in the midst of them the target tower LUDWIG PREUSSER with its unmistakable speedboat hull.

The GRAF ZEPPELIN in the summer of 1940, during its first period at Gotenhafen, here being used as a floating storehouse for the navy's supply of hardwood.

THE POWER SYSTEM

In order to attain the required speed, a steam turbine system driving four shafts, with a total power of 200,000 horsepower, was required. Such a powerful system had never before existed in any ship built in Europe up to this time. The GRAF ZEPPELIN had four turbine units built by Brown, Boveri & Co., each producing 50,000 horsepower individually; her sister ship "B" was to have marine turbines of the same power from the Krupp Germania Shipyards. Steam was produced in sixteen La Mont water-pipe boilers, each operating at a pressure of 75 atmospheres and a temperature of 450 degrees Celsius. Each group of four boilers was housed in a separate boiler room. The turbine units (of which the two forward ones were housed side by side in the same turbine room, while the two aft units were housed in separate rooms, one behind the other) operated four shafts, each with a four-bladed propeller of 4.4-meter diameter. At 300 revolutions per minute, the top speed was to be 34.5 knots (after building on the bulges, it was still to be 33.8 knots). The power-to-weight ratio of the entire system was stated as 19.25 kilograms per horsepower, reckoning on approximately 3850 tons.

A new element in shipbuilding of the time was the Voith-Schneider steering system. Because of the great height of her sides, the GRAF ZEPPELIN had to offer the wind a very large contact area (the air lateral plan—the surface of the longitudinal plane of a ship over her waterline—amounted in her case to about 4500 square meters, approximately the sail area of the full-rigged ship PREUSSEN). This caused the danger of being pushed against the walls of the Kiel Canal by the wind, because the aircraft carrier, like all large ships, would not be easy to control via the rudder at the prescribed speed of 8 knots. Therefore two Voith-Schneider systems of 450 PSe (330 kW) each were installed forward in the ship, one behind the other, arranged so as to be moved into or out of vertical shafts, for the purpose of holding the carrier against the wind. Their pressure was sufficient to move the ship at a speed of 4.5 knots in currentless water with no wind.

This picture, taken at a very acute angle, shows the port side of the carrier with the overhanging positions and mounts for anti-aircraft weapons and other things that were later built on. The supports of the flight deck and the protective shields of the port catapult, installed meanwhile, are clearly seen here.

To provide electrical energy, four generating systems were installed. These included five Diesel generators of 350 kW each (475 HP), five turbo-generators of 460 kW each (625 HP), and one turbogenerator of 230 kW (315 HP), with an attached 200 kVA alternating-current generator. The total capacity amounted to 4280 kW at 220 volts.

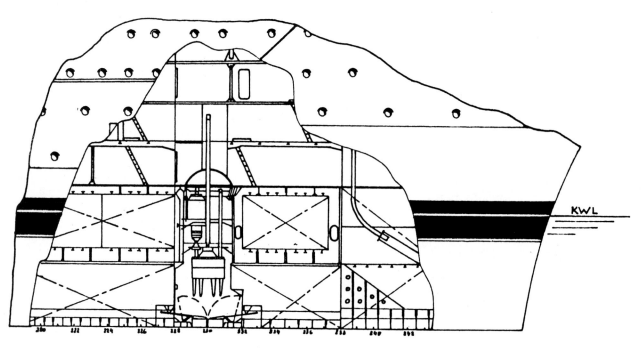

The VS steering system in the bow (cutaway).

The GRAF
ZEPPELIN made
fast at Stettin in
1941; a view of the
bow with the
"Atlantic bow"
rebuilt early in 1939.

Thus did the people of Stettin see the carrier in the summer of 1941. Whoever arrived there by train could recognize it at a long distance.

This picture was
taken from a British
reconnaissance
plane during 1941
and shows the
GRAF ZEPPELIN
at its mooring place
in Stettin.

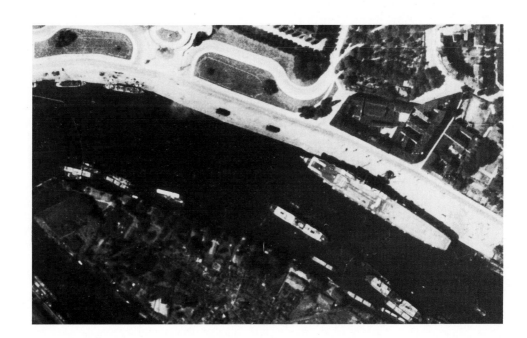

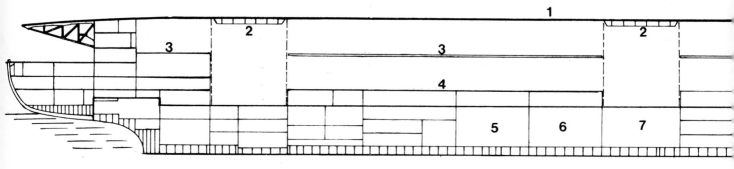

Longitudinal drawing of the ship's hull.
The numbers indicate:

1. Flight deck
2. Aircraft elevator
3. Upper hangar deck
4. Lower hangar deck
5. Turbine room 1
6. Turbine room 2

This picture probably shows the **GRAF ZEPPELIN** setting out on its return trip to Gotenhafen. The mast ends, like those of all large German warships, were telescopic, in order to fit under the bridges of the Kiel Canal.

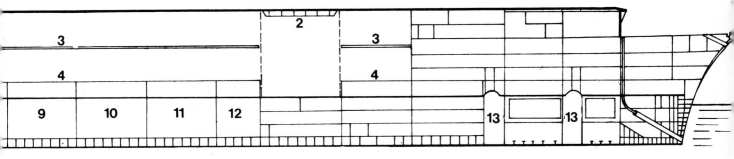

7. Turbine room 3/4
8. Boiler room 1
9. Boiler room 2
10. Boiler room 3
11. Boiler room 4
12. Auxiliary machines
13. VS systems

The **GRAF ZEPPELIN** in harbor basin V during its second period in Gotenhafen, here camouflaged to avoid aerial sighting.

Armament

The artillery weaponry was a point of contention from the start. If the originally planned eight 20.3 cm guns (the armament of a "normal" heavy cruiser), later changed to 15 cm guns, were too much, then so was double that number, as requested by the Naval Weapons Office. This sea-target armament was based on fully false assumptions of the time—and not just in Germany: At that time the aircraft carrier was seen in the role of a support warship, of which it was expected that, when it operated alone, it could defend itself against all possible enemies up to cruisers. On the occasion of a speech by the commander of the navy, Hitler became aware of the problems inherent in this armament. The navy then considered the possibility of doing away with it completely and using additional 10.5 cm anti-aircraft guns instead. But this proved to be im-

possible for technical reasons. At this time, though, an additional 10.5 cm anti-aircraft gun—the farthest forward—was included in the plans.

On the basis of the 1939 plans, the artillery weapons included:

Sixteen 15 cm L/55 C/28 guns in C/36 double mountings in casemate positions, with 115 rounds per gun (1840 rounds in all), Twelve 10.5 cm L/65 G/33 anti-aircraft guns in C/31 double mountings, with 400 rounds per gun (4800 rounds in all), Twenty-two 3.7 cm L/83 C/33 anti-aircraft guns in C/30 double mountings, with 2000 rounds per gun (44,000 rounds in all), and Seven 2 cm L/115 C/30 anti-aircraft guns in (single) C/30 socket mountings, with 2000 rounds per gun (14,000 rounds in all).

Fire Control and Navigational and Other Systems

The sea-target artillery received its firing data from a forward (main) artillery control post and an after (reserve) artillery control post, both located on the island deck. For range measurement, a combined 6-meter long-base device and direction indicator (without a protective housing) was available, plus two target finders. The operation of the 10.5 cm double anti-aircraft guns was done by means of four triaxially stabilized ball-type SL-6 anti-aircraft control posts, of which the three forward ones were equipped with a 4-meter base and the fourth with a 5-meter base. The 3.7 and 2 cm guns each had a

portable 1.25 meter electric measuring device. To illuminate targets there were four floodlights, each about 1.5 meters in diameter; they were located on consoles around the smokestack and at the foremast. Radar measuring devices had been planned since 1937, but no positions for them had been provided in the stages of planning up to 1938-39. In the bow bulge there was an S-device as well as a bow protection device with an extendable shaft. A group listening system was to be used for U-boat surveillance.

The Carrier-Based Aircraft

Since the German aircraft industry could just barely meet the Luftwaffe's needs in developmental work and aircraft production, it was obvious from the start that it would be impossible to develop and build special models of carrier planes, as the needed numbers, even including plentiful spares, were small enough and thus did not seem very attractive to the manufacturers. Thus the Luftwaffe worked with those types already in series production that could be rebuilt for their future use. These changes mainly concerned the (now folding) wings, the installation of hooks for the arrester gear, and certain reinforcements of the frame and the landing gear. A total of up to 43 aircraft were to be carried, including fighters, dive bombers and multipurpose planes. A first experiment to create a carrier fighter

was made with an "Arado 197" biplane, a direct derivative of the available "Arado 68." This version went through its flight testing in 1938-39; since it was shown that the attained top speed of 400 kph was no longer sufficient, this development was halted and the Messerschmitt 109 E, already fully developed, was finally adapted for use as a carrier fighter ("Me 109 T"). A model adapted from the Junkers 87, the "Junkers 87 C", was planned as a dive-bomber; five of these were built and tested by the Travemünde Testing Institute. Multipurpose planes for reconnaissance and torpedo operations were contracted for with the Fieseler and Arado firms, and test models were delivered as early as 1937-38. They were the Fieseler 167 and Arado 195 biplanes. As of 1939-40 these were eliminated.

The "Ju 87-C" equipped with folding wings and landing hook for aircraft carrier service.

Front view of the "Ju 87 C."

The "Me 109 E" was intended to be adapted into a carrier fighter and, as such, to be designated "Me 109 T."

Toward the end of 1942, the GRAF ZEPPELIN was towed to Kiel to be completed. The camouflage mats stretched over the superstructure can be seen here.

Eight weeks after it reached Kiel came the final departure of the GRAF ZEPPELIN. On account of a command issued by Hitler, the work on it had to be halted. When the GRAF ZEPPELIN left Kiel on April 21, 1943 it lacked its two main masts, but the side bulges had already been built on. This picture shows the towing procession, presumably in the Kieler Inneoförde.

Two days later the GRAF ZEPPELIN reached its mooring place on the Mönne, a branch of the Oder near Stettin. There the ship apparently had only half a meter of water under its keel. This picture shows it lying there, the port bulge projecting visibly from the hull.

Another picture taken at the same mooring place, with a view of the carrier's stern. Here the starboard bulge can be seen dimly.

It did not take long for the GRAF ZEPPELIN to be spotted by Allied air reconnaissance. Nevertheless, no air attacks aimed at it seem to have been flown; the enemy probably knew already that the Germans had stopped working on it. This aerial surveillance photo was taken shortly after the ship arrived in the Stettin area.

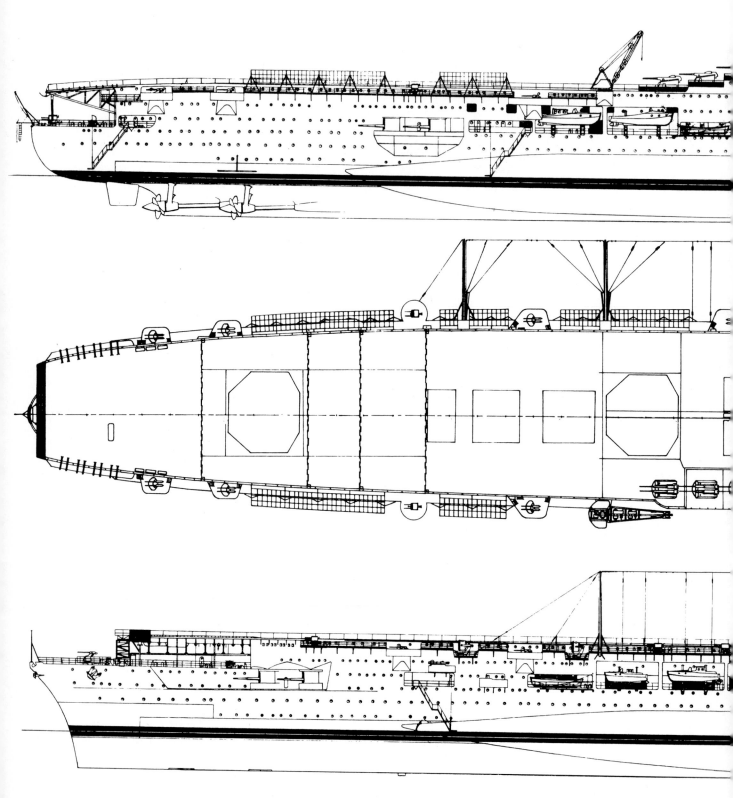

The aircraft carrier GRAF ZEPPELIN according to 1942 planning. From top to bottom: starboard side view with front view beside it at the right, top view, port view of the ship's hull (attachments in mirror-image form).

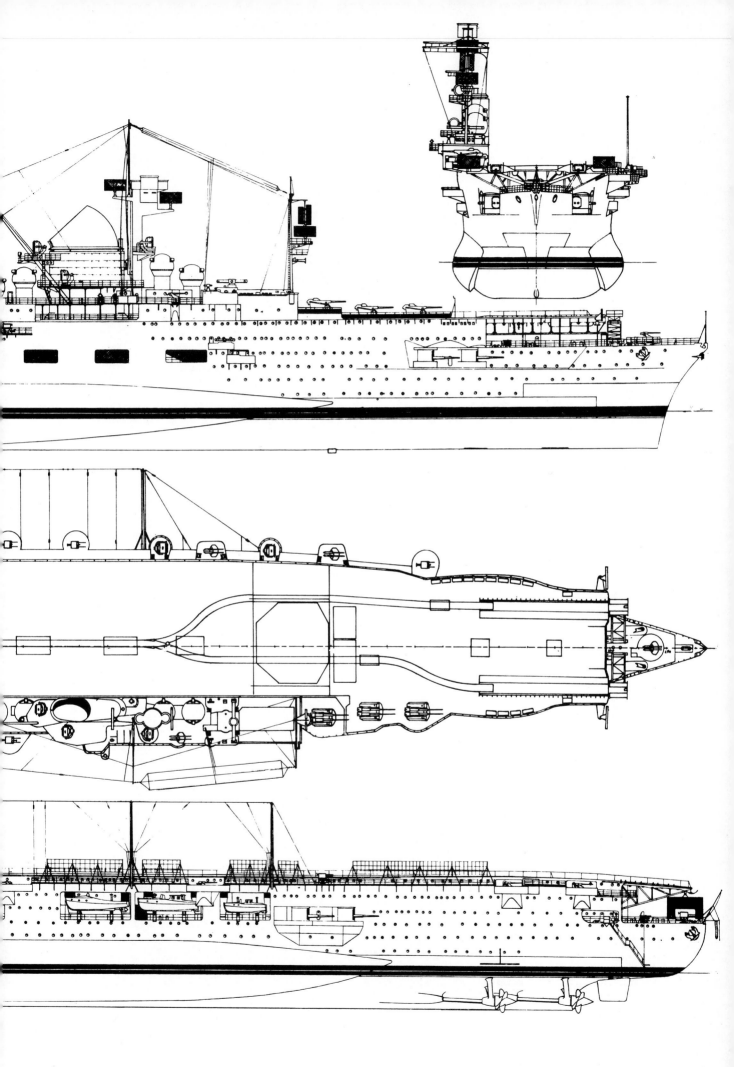

Thus did the Russians find the carrier when they took Stettin. Externally it appeared unharmed, but it was fast on the bottom (which does not show because of the very low depths there), and serious interior damage had been caused by explosions.

This is the last known photograph of the GRAF ZEPPELIN. It was taken on July 26, 1947 at Swinemünde, where the ship was towed after being made watertight and floated. There its hangar decks are said to have been loaded with great quantities of booty. Such materials seem to have been loaded on the flight deck too.

THE FLIGHT SYSTEMS

The airplanes were not, as was common practice on the carriers of other naval powers, to take off from the flight deck, but were to be catapulted, so as to get them into the air as quickly as possible. For that purpose two 23.5 cm compressed-air fast-start catapult tracks, each about 23.5 meters long, were built into the forward part of the flight deck. With these it was theoretically possible to launch all eight planes of a unit within three and a half minutes. They included—since the catapults functioned with launching sleds—very complicated catching and returning devices. The forward-rebounding launching sleds rolled away sidewards on stages and were lowered one deck onto rails under the elevators installed for them, on which they returned to the flight deck to be ready for a new start. On the flight deck there were braking cables at 25.5, 44.5, 54.2 and

66 meters (measured from the zero rib, 5 meters before the point of the stern), four of them in all. There were also erectable wind protectors 3.75 meters high and 13.5 meters long, two of them in all. The **GRAF ZEPPELIN** was constructed as an aircraft carrier with two hangar decks, linked to the flight deck by three elevators. Each of the two hangar decks was about 6.5 meters high and up to 15.5 meters wide; the upper one had a length of barely 185 meters, the lower one of about 170 meters. According to the original plans, the upper hangar deck was to hold 13 Ju 87 C planes (forward) and eight to ten Fi 167 (abaft the aft elevator), while the lower deck was to hold ten Fi 167 (forward) and eight Fi 167 (aft). The supply of aviation fuel was to be between 150 and 200 tons.

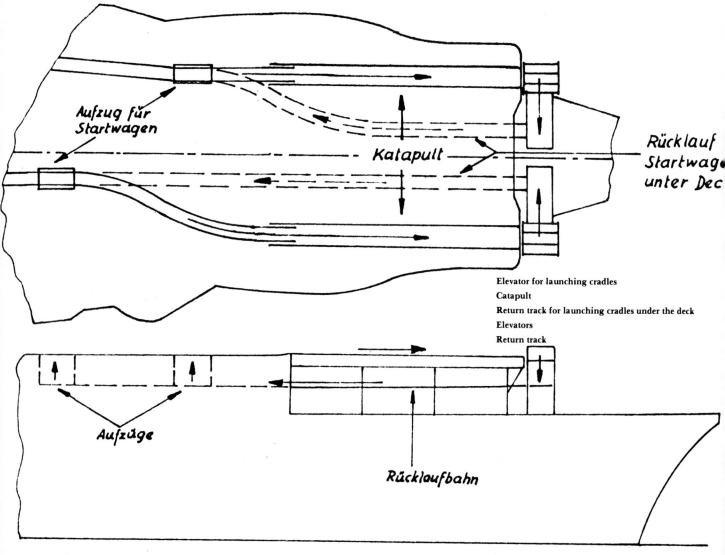

Elevator for launching cradles
Catapult
Return track for launching cradles under the deck
Elevators
Return track

The catapult system.

COMPLETION AFTER ALL?

During the course of the sea war to the end of 1941, the aircraft carrier took on ever-greater significance: British carrier-based planes were able to make a heavy attack on the Italian fleet at Tarento in November of 1940, a chance strike by British torpedo bombers decided the battle against the battleship BISMARCK, and the successful attack of carrier-supported Japanese bombers and torpedo planes against the American fleet at Pearl Harbor made this change in maritime war and its weapons abundantly clear. Thus the lack of their own aircraft carriers was soon seen in Germany as a great disadvantage, and the naval leadership was constantly under pressure to finish the GRAF ZEPPELIN and put it into service. The decisive discussion took place at the Führer's headquarters on April 16, 1942. Its results can be summed up as follows:

1. The work on the ship's hull and machinery—at first just half the powerplant—could be done by the summer of 1943.
2. The use of adapted versions of the aircraft types "Me 109" or "Bf 109" and "Ju 87" as originally planned, the only possibilities considered at that time, made certain modifications of the flight system necessary. Above all, high-powered catapults would be necessary, and their development, construction and testing would require up to two years. The possibility of adapting the existing catapults and making them ready for use was also considered, though, and the space of six months seemed sufficient for this. In view of this situation, the winter of 1943-44 appeared to be the earliest possible time at which the carrier could be completed. The development of a special type of aircraft for carrier use seemed, as the Luftwaffe saw it, not to be possible before 1946.
3. The Luftwaffe at first declared that it was ready to prepare ten fighter planes and twenty-two dive bombers (which were also to be used for reconnaissance). The use of torpedo bombers was given up because of Hitler's attitude that they were not necessary.

Under these conditions, the Naval High Command issued orders on May 13, 1942 for the continued construction and completion of the carrier GRAF ZEPPELIN. Along with the changes in the flight system, there were several other modifications that had become necessary on account of the further development of naval technology since 1938-39. Above all, the structure of the island was no longer sufficient. A heavy mast with a fighter-plane command post in its top and radar equipment had to replace the former staff mast, and the ship's command and weapons control headquarters had to be housed in a shrapnel-proof housing. In addition, a tall funnel was necessary to keep the fighter command post free of smoke. All of this effected a considerable gain in weight, which—to maintain the ship's stability—had to be equalized. For that reason, bulges were built on either side, which primarily had the job of equalizing weight. The port bulge was made of normal ST 52 shipbuilding steel, the starboard bulge of thinner material, 18 mm thick at most. The bulges had a maximum width of 2.4 meters and were attached over the bilge keels. They were partially used as heating-oil bunkers; this allowed an increase in the ship's range, which had previously been considered too short. In addition, the bulges offered the advantage of better protection against underwater weapons, because if a torpedo or mine struck, the center of detonation would be moved farther out.

The originally planned 2 cm single anti-aircraft guns were also no longer sufficient. Instead of them, 2 cm quadruple mounts were called for, with larger supplies of ammunition—now 56,000 rounds compared the former 14,000. As for aircraft, 28 "Ju 87" dive-bombers and twelve "BF 109" fighter planes were now planned for, forty planes in all.

Because of the steadily increasing danger of air attacks, the transfer of the ship, under the false name of "Zander", to Kiel, where the planned work was to be done, was delayed. First the Gotenhafen branch of the Deutsche Werke Kiel AG had to install an armament of three 3.7 cm twin and six 2 cm quadruple guns as well as four anti-aircraft searchlights, so that the ship would be able to defend itself against air attack during the transfer trip. Towed by three tugboats, the GRAF ZEPPELIN left Gotenhafen on November 30, 1942; its escort fleet consisted of three Type 35 minesweepers and six patrol boats. On December 3, 1942 the escort reached the Heikendorf Bay near Kiel, on December 5 it arrived at the Deutsche Werke, where the carrier was immediately docked in a 40,000-ton floating dock and the shipbuilding work (the construction of the bulges) began.

At the same time, work on the machinery commenced, with the goal of making the two inner shafts ready for a speed of 25 to 26 knots. The autumn of 1943 was set as the target for putting the ship in service provisionally; after that, testing was to begin. But all of this never took place. On January 30, 1943 came the "Führer's Command" to take all large units of the navy out of action or halt their construction—in the words of the Commander of the Navy, Grand Admiral Dr. h.c. Raeder, it was "the cheapest sea victory that England ever won" and the reason for his departure. On February 2, 1943 the order to stop work reached the GRAF ZEPPELIN—until March, the only work done was that which would allow pumping by steam pumps in case of a leak.

On April 21 tugs took the carrier in tow, arriving in Stettin two days later. There—with just half a meter of water under its keel—it was moored in the Mönne (an arm of the Oder). Only twice more was the GRAF ZEPPELIN the subject of official discussion: in the spring of 1943 the Ministry of Armament asked whether the carrier could be considered as a transporter of rubber from Japan—rubber was a raw material that was very necessary for the German armaments industry but it was in very short supply—and in the summer of 1944 the conversion of the ship into living quarters for officers' orderlies was considered. Neither of these considerations became reality, because no requirements for them were given.

THE END

The carrier's hour struck after the Red Army had begun the invasion of the Reich. At first the shutoff levers on the pumping system were removed and the ship set on the bottom by flooding. After that, a ten-man special command was ordered to the carrier, to keep in communication with the local naval authorities by radio and prepare to blow up the ship by means of water bombs in the area of the power-plants. At 1800 hours on April 25, 1945, Captain Wolfgang Kähler, empowered by the Commanding Admiral of the Western Baltic Sea in Stettin, gave the command to ignite. This was just before the arrival of the Red Army in the Stettin area. From a shipyard crane in the Vulkan Shipyard in Stettin, Kähler was able to observe the fulfillment of the order; thick clouds of smoke came from the funnel of the GRAF ZEPPELIN—a sign that the charges had ignited. The carrier, already resting on the bottom, had been damaged so seriously that it would be impossible for the Soviets—that was the intention of the German action—ever again to repair the ship and put it to use.

The salvage specialists of the Soviet Navy took until about March of 1946 to make the carrier watertight and capable of floating and tow it to Swinemünde. Subsequently the hangar decks are said to have been loaded with great quantities of looted goods; on August 14, 1947 tugs again took it in tow and set off on an eastern course. Underway it is said to have encountered a minefield during a storm in the Gulf of Finland, but contrary to early postwar reports, it did not sink, but reached Leningrad, where in 1948-49 it was presumably dismantled piece by piece. What remained of it is said to have been sunk by Soviet destroyers in torpedo drills.

STATISTICS*

			after bulges added
Empty displacement	tons	23,140	
Standard displacement	tons	23,200	ca. 24,500
Construction displacement	tons	27,030	28,090
Operational displacement	tons	29,720	33,550
Length at waterline	meters	250.00	
Overall length	meters	262.50[3]	
Width at waterline	meters	27.00	31.50
Draft at construction displ.	meters	7.35	
Draft at operational displ.	meters	7.60	8.50
Side height	meters	22.50	
Flight deck length	meters	244.00	
Flight deck width, maximum	meters	30.00	
Flight deck height over waterline	meters	15.60	
Powerplant performance	WHP	200,000	
Number of shafts		4	
Number of boilers		16	
Speed, planned	knots	35.0	
Cruising speed, planned	knots	34.5	33.8
Minimum speed	knots	15.0	
Heating oil capacity, maximum	cub.mtrs.	5.187	6.740
Fuel oil capacity	cub.mtrs.	119	
Lubricating oil capacity	cub.mtrs.	222	

Heating oil consumption at:
minimum speed[1]   7800 kg/hour
at 19-knot speed[2]   15,200 kg/hour
at cruising speed[2]   56,400kg/hour
Range   sm/knots 8000/19
Supplies (provisions)   7-8 weeks
Crew   1720 + 317 aircraft technical personnel

Weight group percentages

Calculated on the basis of operational displacement: 29,720 tons

Hull	52.3% - ca.	15,540 tons
Machinery	12.8% - ca.	3,805 tons
Auxiliary machines	4.4% - ca.	1,300 tons
Armaments	5.1% - ca.	1,515 tons
Aircraft (with fuel)	2.0% - ca.	600 tons
Equipment	2.7% - ca.	800 tons
Fresh water	1.9% - ca.	565 tons
Drinking water	2.2% - ca.	650 tons
Heating, fuel, lubricating oil	16.6% - ca.	4,945 tons
	100% - ca.	29,720 tons

*Statistics essentially from Hadeler, *Der Flugzeugträger*, Munich 1968.
[1]So-called peacetime cruising
[2]Battle gearing
[3]Before bow reconstruction 257.30 meters
[4]Extended according to greater heating oil capacity; definite statistics not available.

NEW LIFE FOR
AIRCRAFT CARRIER CONSTRUCTION

From the end of the 1940 war year on, German naval leadership concerned itself—at least partially as a result of the successful British carrier-plane attack on the Italian fleet at Tarento—with considerations as to how to remedy the lack of aircraft carriers most quickly. Subjects under discussion concerned not only the reconstruction of existing large warships, but also the adaptation of merchant ships, insofar as they seemed suitable in terms of size and speed. Included in these considerations were the battleships SCHARNHORST and GNEISENAU, as well as the heavy cruisers LUTZOW (ex-pocket battleship "Deutschland") and ADMIRAL SCHEER on the one hand, and the three passenger ships EUROPA, POTSDAM and GNEISENAU of the North German Lloyd line on the other.

The three passenger ships were the only ones that met the basic requirements: the EUROPA was the largest, since the loss of the BREMEN to fire, weighing nearly 50,000 tons, and had a suitable top speed of 27 knots, while the POTSDAM and GNEISENAU, of only about 18,000 tons and a speed of 21 knots, were some what less well-suited though still usable. In addition, the rebuilding of the heavy cruiser SEYDLITZ, about 90% finished, seemed feasible, as opposed to the battleships of the SCHARNHORST class and the heavy cruisers LUTZOW and ADMIRAL SCHEER, which were dropped from these considerations.[1]

The creation of aircraft carriers was one of the main points in the Commander of the Navy's report to Hitler at the latter's headquarters on May 13, 1942. Thereupon Hitler decided that the EUROPA, GNEISENAU and POTSDAM should be rebuilt into auxiliary carriers. In a further report taking place on August 26, 1942 a further possibility was suggested: this involved the French cruiser DE GRASSE, lying on the slipway in Lorient, the rebuilding of which into an aircraft carrier seemed feasible.

The rebuilding plans for these ships were begun at once. In the process it was learned that the task had obviously been strongly underestimated and the difficulties that would necessarily arise in the construction of these ships, intended as they were for fully different purposes, had gone unrecognized. It was chiefly their form and weight stability and their inner division that were insufficient. It was believed that these problems could be mastered by applying a thick "armor plate" of heavy cement and building on side bulges, but this could not be achieved in a really satisfactory way and, in addition, brought about a limitation of their speed, which was not that great to begin with. The EUROPA—now designated "Auxiliary Aircraft Carrier I"—was to be rebuilt by Blohm & Voss in Hamburg—her builders—but this did not transpire: as early as November 25, 1942 the work of planning was halted and the rebuilding was cancelled even before the work had begun. The reason for this was the lack of stability even with the bulges built on, the problem of rigidity caused by the lowering of the hangar deck into the main formation deck, which could not be done any other way, and finally the expected very high fuel consumption when the ship was in use again.

The rebuilding of the other passenger ships was to be entrusted to the naval shipyards at Wilhelmshaven (GNEISENAU) and the Howaldt Works of Hamburg (POTSDAM; what with the cancellation of the rebuilding of the EUROPA, the contract for the POTSDAM was transferred to Blohm & Voss in November of 1942). With them too, problems of a very similar kind arose, especially in terms of stability, which were addressed with the same means—building on bulges and applying heavy concrete "armor plate." But since these measures were, in the end, not able to make much change, the work on the GNEISENAU was halted on November 25, 1942, so that only the POTSDAM remained.

According to a decision made on the same day, this was to be set up as a training aircraft carrier. The work actually began that December: in Kiel they began to remove the passenger cabins. In the midst of this work, it all came to an abrupt end on the basis of the aforementioned "Führer's Command."

The work of planning for the conversion of the uncompleted French heavy cruiser DE GRASSE, which began in April of 1942 under the designation "Auxiliary Aircraft Carrier II", led to this project being given up, as it was shown to be too expensive in terms of work and materials, was under ever-increasing danger of air attack, and finally, second thoughts about what from the German standpoint was an unsatisfactorily divided power system could not be allayed. At the beginning of February 1943 the planning work was halted.

After the spring of 1943 the navy thus had no possibility of any realizable construction of aircraft carriers.

---

[1]The question of rebuilding the SEYDLITZ into an aircraft carrier is treated in a "Naval Arsenal" volume on the heavy cruisers of the ADMIRAL HIPPER class.

The high-speed steamship EUROPA was to be rebuilt into an auxiliary aircraft carrier, but the plans were not to be realized. In the foreground is the EUROPA with camouflage paint. In front of it is the sister ship BREMEN, which fell victim to a fire in March of 1941.

The Auxiliary Aircraft Carrier Projects 1942-43

		EUROPA	POTSDAM	GNEISENAU	de GRASSE
Standard displacement	tons	44,000	17,500	18,160	11,400
Operational displacement	—	56,500	23,500		
Overall length	meters	291.5	203	203.5	192.5
Width over bulges	meters	37	26.8	26.8	24.4
Draft	meters	10.3	8.8	8.8	5.6
Number of power turbines		4	2*	2	2
Number of boilers		24	4	4	4
Propelling power	WHP	105,000	26,000	26,000	110,000
Speed	knots	26.5	21	21	32
Range	knts	5000/27	9000/19	9000/19	7000/19
Number of Ju 87-D planes		18	12	12	12
Number of Me 109-G planes		24	12	12	11
Number of catapults		2	2	2	2
10.5 cm anti-aircraft guns		12	12	12	12
3.7 cm anti-aircraft guns		20	10	10	12
2 cm anti-aircraft guns		28-36	24	24	24

*turboelectric power

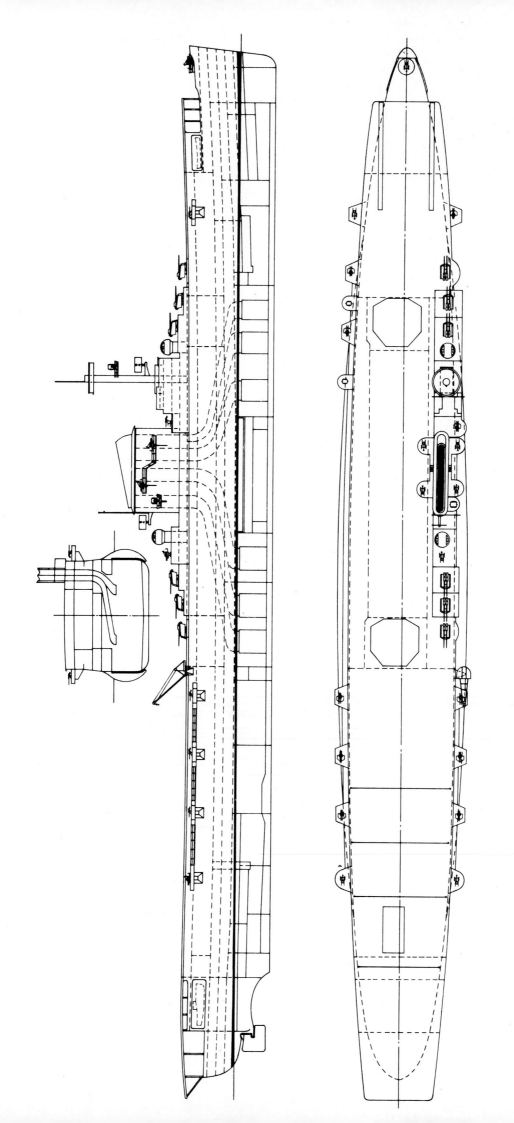

Project "Auxiliary Aircraft Carrier I", the former high-speed steamer EUROPA.

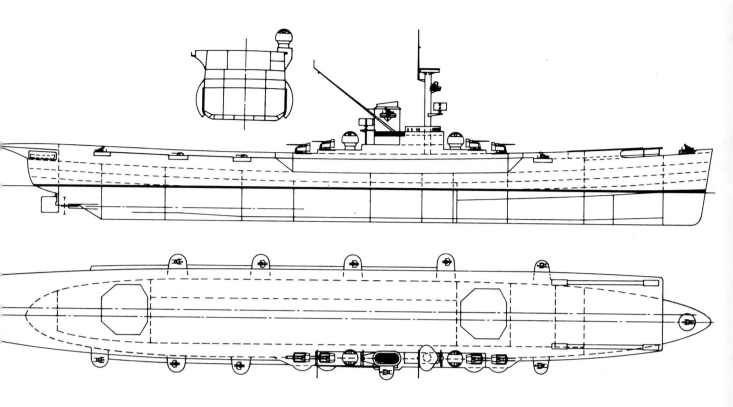

Project "Auxiliary Aircraft Carrier Elbe", the former passenger ship POTSDAM,

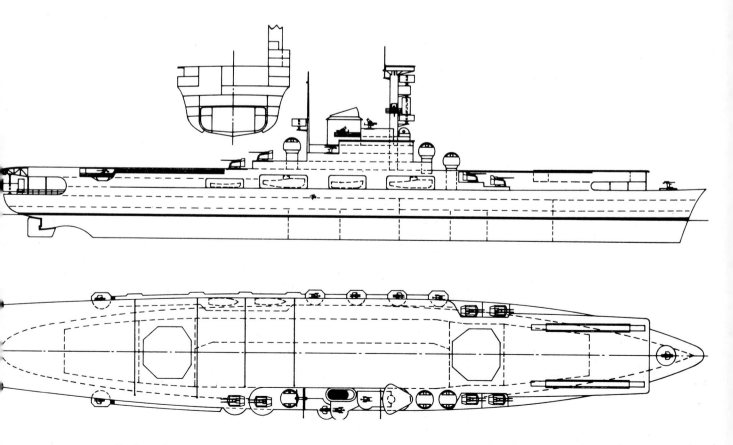

Project "Auxiliary Aircraft Carrier II", the uncompleted French cruiser DE GRASSE.

NAVAL INFO UP-TO-DATE

THE NEWEST ROCKET DESTROYERS
OF THE FRENCH NAVY

There were originally supposed to be four units, but only two of the new French "Corvettes Antiaériennes" of Type "C 70 AA" were actually built, namely the CASSARD and JEAN BART (the names chosen for the other two were COURBET and CHEVALIER-PAUL—these, like the first two, are traditional French naval names). The reason for the limitation is mainly the development of a new aerial defense rocket weapons system (the main armament component of this class). It is supposed to replace the American "Standard SM 1 MR" system and also be capable of action against rockets.

"ASTER 15"—as it is called—will have a range of 15,000 meters and be operational by 1995. The first units to be equipped with it will be three light frigates ("Fregates legères") now in the planning stage, the construction of which is part of the program, which runs until 1991. The CASSARD and JEAN BART will thus be the last units of the "Marine Nationale" to be equipped with the American "Standard SM 1 MR" system. The CASSARD, which has been undergoing testing for several months, is to be put into service in the spring of 1988, and the JEAN BART two years later.

The French rocket destroyer CASSARD on a test run. The spherical housings forward of the funnel serve the satellite communication; the two devices arranged in order of their heights aft of the funnel are fire control components for the ship-to-air rocket weapons system.

The CASSARD seen from dead ahead, from the aircraft observer's point of view. Forward of the bridge complex is the 100 mm rapid-fire cannon, which theoretically can fire 60 rounds a minute.

DETAILS OF THE CASSARD—CLASS

Operational Displacement 4300 tons
Overall length   139 meters
Width   14 meters
Draft   5.5 meters
Power system   4 SEMT-Pielstick 18 PA 6 BTC diesel motors on two shafts with fixed propellers
Performance   31,760 kW (ca. 43,000 HP)
Speed   30 knots
Crew   240
Armament   8 "MM-40" sea-target rockets in 8 individual containers;
                            40 "Standard SM-1 MR" anti-aircraftrockets with one double launcher (for medium distances);
                            2 "SADRAL" anti-aircraft rocket systems for close and closest range);

TB1 100 mm cannon;

                            2 20 mm anti-aircraft machine guns;
                            2 catapult systems for anti-submarinetorpedoes (with 10 "L 5" anti-submarine torpedoes);
                            1 light sub-chasing helicopter.

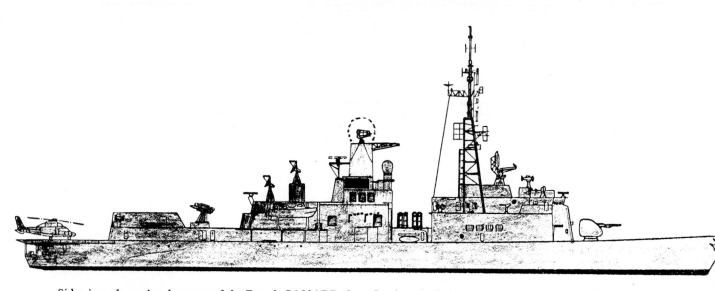

Side view of a rocket destroyer of the French CASSARD class. On the raised electronic tower between the funnels, a dotted line indicates the outline of the radar dome, which is still lacking.

RUMANIA'S AMBITIOUS FLEET EXPANSION

After a long period of cooperation with the People's Republic of China in marine technology, marked only by insignificant developments and now at an end, action has newly taken place in Rumania's fleet expansion. This obviously became possible after, in the course of a strongly favored industrial expansion, a shipyard for naval shipbuilding had been built at Mangalia, which has been capable of production since the end of the Seventies. What might be called the "shining example" of the developments underway since then is the rocket destroyer MUNTENIA, launched on August 5, 1985 in the presence of party leader and chief of state Ceaucescu (a second ship is reported to be under construction). This does not appear to be—as was originally expected—a copy of a Soviet model, built under license, but rather an independent Rumanian contribution within the parameters of the Warsaw Pact; its success was, though, contributed to by Soviet deliveries of weapons and electronic systems.

The MUNTENIA appears to be a very independently designed type of surface warship designed for high-seas fleet operations, its high-rising hull and no less high superstructures making it look quite out of the ordinary.

Data and details of the MUNTENIA:

Operational displacement	5000-6000 tons
Overall length	145 to 148 meters
Width	16 meters
Power system	COGAG gas turbines or CODAG gas turbines and Diesel motors
Number of shafts	two
Speed	28 to 32 knots
Armament	4 x 2 launch containers for "SS-N-2C" sea-target rockets;
	7(?) x 4 launchers for "SA-N-5" anti-aircraft rockets;
	2 x 2 76 mm guns;
	2 x 3 anti-submarine torpedo tubes;
	2 x 16 anti-submarine "RBU-2500" rocket launchers;
	2 helicopters ("Alouette-3"?).
Electronics	1 "Strut Curve" air-space panoramic-search radar;
	1 navigational radar;
	1 "Owl Screech" fire-control device;
	2 "Drum Tilt" fore control devices;
	Eloka, sonar.

The four (or only three?) frigates of the "Tetal" class are also recent. They too were built at Mangalia and have presumably been operational since 1983. They likewise represent an independently developed type, though their weapons and electronic systems have been helped by Soviet-provided equipment; like the MUNTENIA, they are characterized by high hulls and superstructures. Other than photographs taken more or less from forward, there is as yet no pictorial material on these units. For that reason, any evaluations to date can have only a temporary nature and must be taken with all reservations.

The militarily relevant data on the "Tetal" class:

Operational displacement	1800 to 1900 tons
Overall length	93 to 95 meters
Width	11.5 meters
Power system	Diesel motors
Number of shafts	two
Speed	? knots

Armament	2 x 2 76 mm guns;
	2 x 2 30 mm anti-aircraft guns;
	2 x 2 14.5 mm anti-aircraft machineguns;
	2 x 2 anti-submarine torpedo tubes;
	2 x 16 "RBU-2500" anti-submarine rocketlaunchers;
	1 helicopter.
Electronics	1 "Strut Curve" air-space panoramic search radar;
	1 navigational radar;
	1 "Drum Tilt" weapons control device;
	1 "Owl Screech" weapons control device.

Side view of the rocket destroyer MUNTENIA.

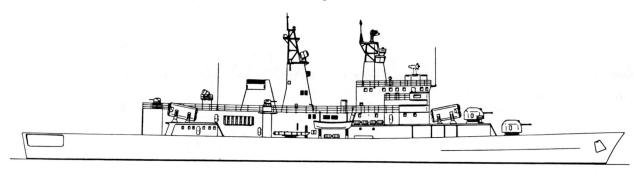

Perspective drawing of the MUNTENIA.

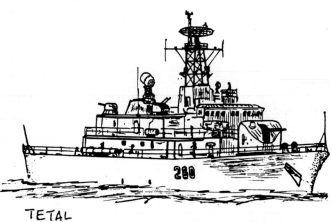

Perspectivistic drawing of a frigate of the "Tetal" class.

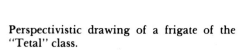

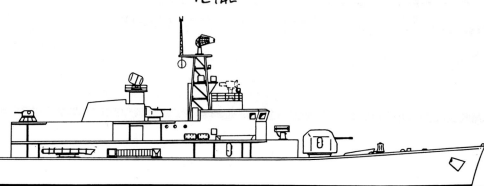

A side view of the "Tetal" class might look like this.

THE MULTIPURPOSE BOATBUILDING PROGRAM OF THE FEDERAL GERMAN NAVY

Because the majority of the testing craft of the Federal German Navy are overage, the construction of replacements has been agreed on since 1978-80 and included in a building program which has now begun to be developed. This program assures the influx of a type family of so-called "Multipurpose boats" (MZB); these are not, though, supposed to replace individual older craft ready to be disposed of. Rather they are so designed that they can be used for a number of testing tasks by using "equipment sets." Their numbers will thus be kept smaller than the present number of obsolete craft. Three basic types are coming into being:

—The "Multipurpose Boat Large" (MZB gross), as the so-called "Class 749" in two variations: Type A for torpedo testing and Type B for sonar testing. At first two units are being built: the Type A craft is to be begun in 1989. At this time the following para-meters are being utilized: Operational displacement approximately 1750 tons, overall length 75 meters, width 12.5 meters, draft 3.7 meters.

—The "Multipurpose Boat Medium" (MZB mittel) as "Class 748." Three boats have been ordered, their data being given as follows: Operational displacement approximately 1000 tons, overall length 56.5 meters, width 10.8 meters, draft 3.65 meters; Diesel-electric power producing 1905 kW (approx. 1490 HP) for a speed of 12.7 knots. The three craft contracted for with the Kröger Shipyards in Rendsburg are:

SCHWEDENECK (NATO registration Y 860), delivery date October 1987,
KRONSORT (NATO registration Y 861), delivery date December 1987,
HELMSAND (NATO registration Y 862), delivery date February 1988.

Multipurpose boat SCHWEDENECK, built by the Kröger Shipyards in Rendsburg.

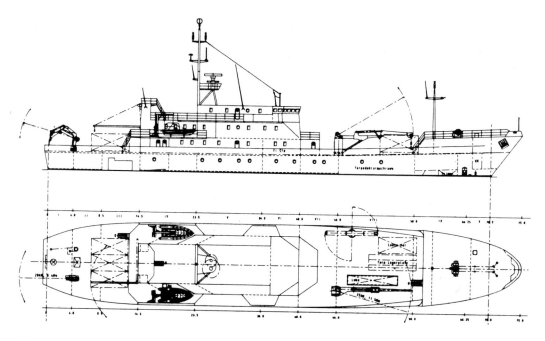

The "Multipurpose Boat Large" as presently planned.

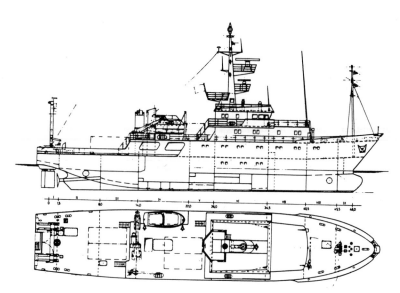

The "Multipurpose Boat Medium" as it has been built.

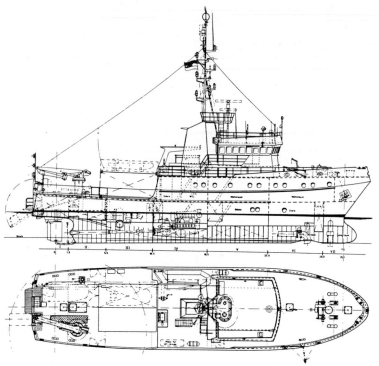

The planned "Multipurpose Boat Small."

—The "Multipurpose Boat Small" (MZB klein), as "Class 751." Five units are being built, their contracts being given in the winter of 1987-88 to a shipyard consortium that consists of the Lürssen Shipyards in Vegesack, the Kröger Shipyards in Rendsburg and the Elsfleth Shipyards AG. According to the original plans, the Kröger and Elsfleth yards were each to build two boats and the Lürssen yards one, but changes are still possible, as possible solutions are presently being sought that would be more economical; one possibility, for example, is the construction of identical sections in each shipyard (as the mine boats of Class 343, expected soon, are being built). The delivery dates for the Elsfleth yards are the autumn of 1989 and the beginning of 1990. The following parameters have been stated for these boats: Operational displacement approximately 440 tons, overall length 36 meters, width 9 meters, draft 2.75 meters; power system producing 800 kW (about 1100 HP) for a speed of 12 knots. These five boats are to replace five old torpedo boats, one diving tender and one radar boat.

No armament is planned for any of these boats, because they are to be used exclusively in the realm of the so-called "Rü-Fleet"—meaning craft intended for the area of equipment and subordinate to the Federal Office of Defensive Technology and Supply (BWB).

The multipurpose boat KRONSORT, built by the Elsfleth Shipyards.

FROM NAVAL HISTORY

The Origins of the Washington Fleet Conference

On February 6, 1922 a treaty was signed in Washington that left its mark on the history of efforts for peace and can be regarded in terms of its results—regardless of the very different armaments—as equal in value to SALT-I, SALT-II and the medium-range weapons agreement made at the end of 1987. For the first time success was attained at high levels in agreeing on and achieving a general arms reduction. The treaty signatories were then the five leading sea powers in the world—Great Britain, the USA, Japan, France and Italy. The treaty's roots went back to World War I: while the building of battleships in Europe had almost completely stopped just after the war broke out, the two Pacific sea powers made the best of the situation for their own purposes. Undisturbed by the events in Europe, they could continue to build battleships and even force the pace.

In developing Japan, 1916 was the year in which the so-called "8/8 Program" was adopted (it included the building of eight battleships and eight battle cruisers, foreseeing the future existence of 24 such units) and immediately begun. In so doing, Japan at once overstepped the previous caliber limit of 38.1 cm and armed its new major warships with 40.6 cm cannons, the largest that had ever existed. This threatened to make Japan a great danger to the "Great Entente", especially for the USA, which began to be concerned about its spheres of influence in East Asia. For that reason the American government decided, even during the war, to increase its navy by ten battleships and six large battle cruisers—this was to create a fleet "second to none." The intention of superseding Great Britain, which had maintained its rank as the world's first sea power for more than a century, was clear.

Naturally the British construction policy could not remain unmoved by this. On the one hand, the Japanese position of power in the Far East was just as unpleasant to the British as to the Americans—both had to fear the effect of the rapidly expanding Japanese export industry on their former export markets—and on the other hand, the American fleet threatened to become so strong that it would take over the leading role, formerly that of the Royal Navy, of the world's strongest sea power, and thereby shatter Great Britain's worldwide prestige. For that reason the British Parliament made the funds

available to build, at first, four large battle cruisers with 40.6 cm cannons, as an "answer" to the American and Japanese developments.

In addition, plans were made for even stronger ships, which were to be armed with 45.7 cm cannons. The reason for this further increase in caliber was the attitude of Japan, which strove to retain and strengthen its newly-gained position in the world through naval weapons and was ready to arm a new series of battleships with guns of this heaviest caliber. Thus a new arms race had begun; its end was not in sight, and it would place heavy new financial burdens on the involved powers. At the end of 1921 no fewer than 28 large warships lay on the slipways of American, British and Japanese shipyards, adding up to a total tonnage of more than a million tons, and further, even larger and stronger ships were in various stages of planning.

Despite all that, Great Britain—financially exhausted after the Great War and in need of a stable period of recovery—tried to ease the growing tensions in a peaceful way. For this reason, Foreign Minister Lord Curzon urged the American ambassador in London to have a general conference for the mutual agreement of all involved powers. Far-seeing American officials had also recognized that the goal of this ongoing construction of capital ships could scarcely be reached without causing an American-British fleet rivalry. Then too—and this may have been more decisive—the Americans had to realize that in the near future it would be necessary either to devote an additional, and scarcely less high, amount of money, materials and time enlarging the Panama Canal locks to make them big enough for the coming super-battleships, or to drop out of the arms race and remain only the third greatest sea power, behind Great Britain and Japan. In addition, it had to be taken into consideration that the great expenses involved would be difficult to justify politically after the burdens of the war.

The Americans were not alone in having such misgivings. Most of the other states had similar views, since they too—in some cases considerably more—had been "bled." That was why the American public—capably led by the press—vigorously attacked and questioned the whole idea of a new super-battleship fleet. On the other hand, it was also seen that the Japanese position of power in East Asia

Six of these 43,200-ton, 23-knot battleships of the SOUTH DAKOTA class had been begun in America in 1920. They were to be armed with twelve 40.6 cm guns in four triple turrets as well as 16 15.2 cm guns as medium artillery. All ships of this class were broken up on the slipways as a result of the Washington Fleet Conference.

The "non plus ultra" of American warship construction at that time were the 43,500-ton battle cruisers of the LEXINGTON class, likewise six in number, whose keels were laid in 1920 and 1921. With their 33-knot speed, they would become the fastest large warships in the world. Their armament was to consist of eight 40.6 cm guns in four twin turrets and 16 15.2 cm guns as medium artillery. On the basis of the treaty, four ships were broken up on the slipways; two others—the LEXINGTON and SARATOGA—were rebuilt as aircraft carriers (see also page 8).

The high point of Japanese capital ship planning consisted of four 47,500-ton, 30-knot battleships, to be finished by 1927; their main armament was to be eight 45.7 cm guns plus medium artillery.

was not to be stopped by an arms race. Japan seemed willing to make any sacrifice to carry out its planned naval expansion and achieve its goals. The idea of limiting the Japanese fleet through appropriate treaties and agreements thus seemed more and more alluring. And the time for such negotiations was unusually favorable: the sudden end of the economic boom that had developed quickly during the war had caused a high unemployment rate and a serious economic crisis in Japan, so that the internal political situation was very tense there. It was not difficult to see that the future financial burdens and the political effects resulting from any naval arms race would drive the government, more or less quickly but inevitably, onto a road of no return.

So all involved sea powers welcomed US President Harding's query to Great Britain, Japan, France and Italy in the summer of 1921, as to whether they would accept an invitation to a disarmament conference—all of them declared that they were ready. This conference then began in November of 1921 and lasted three months. The powers agreed and the naval arms race was halted.

The result of these negotiations went down in the history of disarmament efforts as the "Washington Fleet Agreement" and, for the first time, signified a victory of reason over all ambitions for plans to increase military power.

The Japanese YAMATO—seen here shortly before its sinking on April 7, 1945—was the largest and most heavily armed battleship in the world. It was built after Japan had renounced the Washington agreement in 1934.